DEAR PROFESSOR

"Like examples from an ethics textbook, these e-mails from missing students ask for an exception to the rule, and thereby throw all rules into question, sometimes while simultaneously admitting that no exception should be granted. These at times Kafkaesque confessions, woven from desperation and indifference, honesty and concealment, force the instructor into a courtroom to cast judgment on life itself. In the end, a strangely funny and exasperating — sometimes even traumatizing— collection from artist-professor Filip Noterdaeme."

— C. E. Emmer, Emporia State University

"In his latest work, homoplagiarist Filip Noterdaeme documents the dislocations of American education in the digital age. As much a work of sociology as of poetry, Dear Professor gives voice to the voiceless in every classroom discussion: the absent student. The result is a portrait — at once hilarious and haunting and highly instructive — of a new lost generation. Lost not in the trenches at Marne Verdun Namur or Mons, but lost on their way to class."

— Geoffrey Rees, University of Chicago

"If only *Dear Professor* were required reading for all of academia. With his signature wit, Filip Noterdaeme offers us a concise and original exposé of what ails American higher education. My gut ached laughing so hard at this insouciant commentary."

— Rich Benjamin, author of *Searching for Whitopia: An Improbable Journey to the Heart of White America*

Before you start to read this book, take this moment to think about making a donation to punctum books, an independent non-profit press

@ https://punctumbooks.com/support

If you're reading the e-book, you can click on the image below to go directly to our donations site. Any amount, no matter the size, is appreciated and will help us to keep our ship of fools afloat. Contributions from dedicated readers will also help us to keep our commons open and to cultivate new work that can't find a welcoming port elsewhere. Our adventure is not possible without your support.
Vive la open-access.

Fig. 1. Hieronymus Bosch, *Ship of Fools* (1490–1500)

First published in 2016 by dead letter office, BABEL Working Group
an imprint of punctum books, Earth, Milky Way.
https://punctumbooks.com

The BABEL Working Group is a collective and desiring-assemblage of scholar–gypsies with no leaders or followers, no top and no bottom, and only a middle. BABEL roams and stalks the ruins of the post-historical university as a multiplicity, a pack, looking for other roaming packs with which to cohabit and build temporary shelters for intel-lectual vagabonds. We also take in strays.

ISBN-13: 978-0-9982375-8-9
ISBN-10: 0-9982375-8-2
Library of Congress Cataloging Data is available from the Library of Congress

Cover image: Dr. Shuki Cohen
Book design: Vincent W.J. van Gerven Oei

Dear Professor
A Chronicle of Absences

*Collected Emails from College Students
Too Busy to Attend Class*

By Filip Noterdaeme

With an epilogue by Dr. Shuki Cohen

*This book is for my students who teach me much
and for Daniel who teaches me the rest.*

"We convince by our presence."
— Walt Whitman

Contents

Author's Preface

Like many artists and writers in New York City, I teach to make a living. As of this writing, I am an adjunct professor in three major universities, teaching art history to undergraduate students as well as a fair sprinkling of adults and senior citizens who wish to brush up on their general knowledge and understanding of art.

The following anthology compiles a selection of over two hundred emails I received from students in the past few years in which they excuse, justify, or explain their non-attendance in class. Taken together, they paint a staggering portrait of university life in the digital age where missing class is frequently glossed over by an endless string of virtual exchanges that have nothing to do with serious study and learning. Judging from these, at turns candid, beseeching, sometimes even curt or sly emails, it would appear that the American college student of the twenty-first century feels entitled to succeed without really trying.

And yet, re-examining this overwhelming accumulation of epistolary apologies, I cannot help feeling increasingly empathetic towards those who wrote them. Their affected courtesy cannot hide a host of insecurities and sense of isolation, consumed as they are by constant distraction, craving connection yet unable to sustain it. I wish my absentee students would understand that their apologies for missing in action are not my concern. What does matter and what they themselves should be concerned about is that they are missing in on the action.

— Filip Noterdaeme

A Word to the Reader

All emails presented in this book are listed in the chronological order in which they were received. Their style and content (including any spelling mistakes and typos) have been kept intact, with the exception of the form of address, which has been altered to the default "Dear Professor" in order to echo the book's title. All subject lines have been omitted. To protect the writers' identities, all names have been changed and any references to universities and course titles obscured. In some rare cases, confidential private disclosures have been obscured as well.

Dear Professor

9/14/2010

Dear Professor,

I arrived a bit late to the met last Friday and missed check in. I was also not here the first class. I did however complete the assignment at the Met and have typed up my experience, I also stayed at the museum till 5:00 and checked out the modernist wing (my most favored wing). I am prepared to discuss my experience this upcoming Friday. I just wanted to let you know that I am still here and actively participating. I understand if my absence is penalized. See you on Friday :)

best,
Kathey P.

9/16/2010

Dear Professor,

I'm writing to let you know that I won't be in class tomorrow. My band was given the opportunity to play a festival in Vancouver this Friday and Saturday, and so I will be in Canada until this Monday. I saw that you finished the syllabus, and I'm concerned about the short response regarding the Met due tomorrow. I underwent the whole exercise and have a number of notes and passages I wrote down while performing my 'following.' Will it be possible for me to turn these in w/ my absence? Can I hand the short response in when I am in class next Friday? Or would you allow me to e-mail it if it can't be delivered next week?

Obviously, I understand if my unexcused absence simply means I won't get credit for this paper. The bizarre scheduling, bureaucracy, and holidays surrounding the first weeks along with the unfinished syllabus made it difficult for me to get wholly organized. After my absence tomorrow I will be consistently present and engaged with the coursework.

Let me know what I should do (if anything) regarding the Met response and I will see you next week.

Thanks for your time,
Mitchel W.

9/17/2010

Dear Professor,

I am unable to attend class today because I unfortunately have pink eye. I've just seen my doctor and am not allowed out for the next day or so. I have a note explaining my absence and will bring it to you next week. Also, what are your office hours? If possible, I'd like to meet with you to discuss what I've missed.

Thank you,
Iris

9/17/2010

Dear Professor,

I want to apologize for not being able to attend class today. I have a fever and have been unable to attend class this week. I would really like to start this semester on the right foot and not fall behind. I would really appreciate it if you could email me a syllabus as well as any assignments that have already been given to the class. Also, because I am a ████████████ student not a part of ██████████ I need your permission to be officially enrolled in this class. If you would like to meet and discuss this I am available next week. Thank you so much and I look forward to seeing you next Friday.

Best Regards,
Adriana E.

9/19/2010

Cher professeur,

Je ne suis pas venue vendredi dernier en classe. Je pensais que
████████████ était fermé pour Kippour. J'ai découvert en
regardant mes mails à la fin de Kippour qu'il y avait bel et bien
classe ce jour-là. Je vous aurais envoyé un mail auparavant si
j'avais su. J'en suis désolée.

Voici en attachement mon devoir.

Bien à vous,

Justine

Dear Professor,

I didn't make it last Friday to class. I thought ████████████
*was closed for Yom Kippur. I found out while checking my emails
at the end of Kippur that there actually was a class on that day.
Had I known this beforehand, I would have emailed you earlier.
I'm sorry.*

Here attached is my homework.

Best,
Justine

9/29/2010

Dear Professor,

I apologize for my absence last Friday, I was very ill. I would have informed you the day before, but I was quite incapacitated with a fever. I do understand this is an unexcused absence due to me not giving you notice, and that 2 of these mandate a reduction is letter grade. I will see you on Friday at the Guggenheim with all of the assigned handouts read.

warm regards and apologies,
Miguel P.

9/29/2010

Dear professor,

Last monday, I was involved in an accident and broke my collar bone. I will be on bed rest for the next two weeks at least and will be unable to attend class. That said I will do anything and everything in my power to not fall behind in my school work. Is there a way I could keep up with the in class material online? Are there assignments I can do at home and email to you or show you when I am more mobile? Please let me know.

Thank you,
Iris

9/30/2010

Dear Professor,

Sorry I missed the last class. I flew home to LA for my moms wedding! Anyway, are there any particular readings we will be going over in class tomorrow?

Drew

10/7/2010

Dear Professor,

I saw my doctor yesterday and had a follow up x ray and I will be able to start school again on Monday. I will not be in class tomorrow but will be next Friday. I have been following up with the readings and such, but what more should I do to stay on track. I received your email about the paper. Is the hand out you gave in class on blackboard?

Thank you,
Iris

10/11/2010

Dear Professor,

im emailing to inform you of the reason of my absence in class last friday. On my way to the Guggenheim Museum I stopped at school to print out my essays. In a small bit of a rush, and no metro card i opened up the utility door to the metro without paying. A police officer saw me and arrested me, putting me in jail at downtown booking for over forty hours. It was an extremely awful and unnecessary measure I believe, even though the action i was doing was illegal, I believed the worst that could happen was a ticket. I was extremely upset i could not re-turn in my original paper and the latest as well. Here is proof that i have done it , and i will bring in the hard copy next friday. Thank you for understanding.

Sincerely,
Marlon

10/22/2010

Dear Professor,

Sorry I missed class today, I caught the flu thats been going around and have been out of commission since Wednesday. Im bummed I didnt get to join the class for the galleries we were attending today. How much longer will these exhibits be open?

Best,
Drew

10/27/2010

Dear Professor,

I have been confined to my bed for the past week with a nasal and trackia infection (and yes, I have a doctors note). I wasnt able to visit the exhibit this week. I know we have a paper due this friday and I wanted to know if there was an alternate assignment I could do instead. Let me know, if I dont hear back. I suppose we can figure it out after class.

Best,
Drew

10/29/2010

Dear Professor,

I am sick today and I will not be able to come to school. I have tried to push myself to come jusqu'à maintenant où j'abandonne.

Merci de votre compréhension,
Justine

11/1/2010

Dear Professor,

I do hope this note finds you well! Please excuse my absence on Friday last. According to the last email, I read up on the Barnes Foundation, as well as a few other articles you had given us previously. Is there an assignment due on Friday? What more can I do for Friday's class, to ensure I am on track and up to speed? Also, I think I will be taking ████████████ next semester. Is this primarily under class persons, or a solid mix? Talk soon!

Thanks,
Sharon L.

11/12/2010

Dear Professor,

I unfortunately will not be able to make it to class today, but will make sure to see the Alternative Histories exhibit at Exit Art before next class. Is there another exhibition I will have missed and should make sure to see?

Very sorry to be missing class,
Loyd

11/12/2010

Dear Professor,

I do apologize for the late notice, and for my absence, as I have been incapacitated for a 1½ days with the stomach flu. Most unfortunately, I missed the visit to Exit Art with you all. I shall visit before the week is out, in hopes of contributing to any amount of conversation on the place. I will continue to work on Wittgenstein's Mistress as well.

Talk soon.
Sharon

11/30/2010

Dear Professor,

Hopefully, this note finds you well rested after this Thanksgiving holiday break. I wanted to check in with you, regarding our exhibition review assignment. Is this officially due Friday? We are to do a relatively brief write-up for five different exhibitions, correct? I think I was absent the day you communicated all of the information for this piece so, forgive my unawareness.

Talk soon!
Sharon

12/8/2010

Dear Professor,

I was absent last friday do to an opportunity to shoot for New York Magazine. I just wanted to send you the link! I am really excited about it.

all the best,
Kristie

12/10/2010

Dear Professor,

Today, I have a job interview and will be a bit late coming into class. Wanted to let you know.

See you soon!
Sharon

12/17/2010

Dear Professor,

I'm sorry for the late notice but I will not be able to make class today. I have to be at my apartment because I am moving out today. I didn't realize it would conflict with class time. I have attached my paper to this email but if you need me to get a hard copy to you I can figure that out as well. Again, I am sorry for the late notice and thank you for your time this semester.

–Pamela

12/23/2010

Dear Professor,

I have been sick with strep, but I never received confirmation that you received my final which I placed in your mailbox. I have attached copies in this email. Please confirm that you received my final from your mailbox :) I hope you are enjoying holiday and merry Christmas!

best,
Kristie

1/28/2011

Dear Professor,

I apologize for missing today's class, I woke up with a horrible stomach ache (never eating pre-packaged sushi again!). I want to know if I could meet you during your office hours next week to introduce myself and pick up a copy of the syllabus.

Best,
Bruce O.

2/12/2011

Dear Professor,

Wanted to apologize for my absence this week, and for this late note regarding it. Please expect me at the Guggenheim on the 18th. Did you make it to the Douglas Crimp talk? I am going to research that discussion, and perhaps I will find notes or some other publication. Anyways, hope you are well this weekend.

As ever,
Sharon

2/17/2011

Dear Professor,

I am having some issues with one of my teeth and the only dentist appointment i could get this week was tomorrow at 12:00. i hoping that the appointment will not take long i would like to be in class.but in the invites that i do not make it to class I wanted to let you know before head of the situation. i will make sure to bring in documentation of my doctors appointment.

Thank You
Sheila W.

2/18/2011

Dear Professor,

i when i arrived today at the Guggenheim i could not find you or the group. but despite not find the group i spent some time looking around. i will bring a documentation from my doctor to our next class.

Have a safe trip
Sheila W.

2/18/2011

Dear Professor,

Sorry to send this last minute but I had to go into the doctors today for emergency. I had to get stitched up in my left arm because of a benign tumor. It was bothering me this morning and fevering up. I can have a doctors note for you.

But I did check out the exhibit this week and we'll go tomorrow for the new installations that I missed.

I apologize to notify you this late, I had a hectic morning and just now got out of the hospital.

Thank you,
Gloria

2/24/2011

Dear Professor,

Liza and I are enrolled in the ████████████ with you for Fridays (2–4.30 pm) Unfortunately we will miss the opening exercises that first day (Mar 4)

Thanks so much and looking forward to going around with you again

Blake C.

3/3/2011

Dear Professor,

I just found out that I have a medical appointment tomorrow morning that I can't reschedule so I won't be able to make it to class tomorrow. Here's my paper, hope you enjoy. Have a nice weekend!

Best,
Marilyn

3/4/2011

Dear Professor,

I'm still homesick recovering from my surgery.
I was able to make it to my other classes but couldn't take one more day.
sorry to have missed – I have doctor's notes to accommodate this absence.

thus– I did complete the response paper (attached)

thank you,

Gloria

3/9/2011

Dear Professor,

It has been brought to my attention there was a paper due last Friday 04 March, at which time I was ill. Is it permissible to submit this work on Friday 11 March instead? Though it has been difficult narrowing down one central idea, and it seems that many more [ideas] are being abandoned..I am so sorry for the misunderstanding, and I am quite looking forward to class this week. Hopefully this note finds you happy and healthy, and feeling good after the closing of I Love the Contemp...– Loves Me exhibition.

Talk soon,
Sharon L.

3/11/2011

Dear Professor,

I can not afford to make today's trip. I am in a really tight spot right now and hope you understand.
Please let me know if there is there any sort of make-up assignment I can do.

Best,
Bruce O.

3/25/2011

Dear Professor,

I'm feeling really ill today and decided against coming to class. However, I know that we have an assignment ("Director's Pitch") due today, please let me know if you would prefer me to email it in to you or just bring a hard copy with me next class…
I hope you had a great break and i'll see you in class next week

Sincerely,
Viki

3/25/2011

Dear Professor,

I couldn't make it to class today because I had to visit my grandmother at her residency. I forgot that it was my turn to visit her in my family schedule so I apologize if I notified you at this time. However, I did complete response #2 and is attached in this email.

Thank you for understanding sir.
Kristie

3/28/2011

Dear Professor,

This morning my Grandmother died in Athens, Greece, where my family originates. I know that I have missed three classes and to attend the funeral I would have to miss Friday :(. As having a high standing in your class is of the utmost importance to me I wanted to run this by you. I know that there is a paper due Friday would it be possible to email it to you and then place in your mailbox next Monday? and/or extra credit to make up for this missed class?

thank you,
Kristie

3/29/2011

Dear Professor,

I apologize for my absences, it's just that a lot of things has been happening regarding my family and health that took mostly my weekends in the past weeks.

I'll be sure to be more succinct with this class no matter what. sorry to disappoint you professor.

best,
Leena L.

4/3/2011

Dear professor,

I am very sorry for the absence on April 1st. I was in deep con-
dolence of my friend Grace and her family. I have none much
to say right now because I'm going through an emotional state.
Just wanted to inform you now that I'm feeling much better sir.

with much appreciation, thank you.
–Leena L.

5/6/2011

Dear Professor,

So sorry to have missed class today. As it happens, I have bronchitis. Which written works would you like for me to complete? I think I'm behind, but i'm not entirely sure..completed
my course evaluation: you have passed, with flying colors, mr.
noterdaeme! hope you are smiling

Sharon

5/10/2011

Dear Professor,

Hello, my name is Rosie and I'm Leena L.'s cousin. I'm writing on behalf of Leena and contacting the rest of her professors for her friday class because of her current condition.

I would appreciate if you can keep this confidential and in contact with yourself, Leena, and her counselo. She recently was admitted to go to Switzerland on the weekends since about 3–4 weeks ago because of her father's diplomacy and family claim. Every weekend since May 15th Leena had to go to Europe due to her father's reasons and safety being examined for gov't purposes.

She is restricted to use any communication till May 13th because she is currently being monitored by her father's hazard. Thus because I am not of her father's side I am able to contact you on behalf of her. She reached out to me about a week ago to inform her professors. I apologize if I'm writing to you so late and causing any miscommunication of her absences. She will be returning back to the US tomorrow and we'll be in attendance to your class this week.

She kindly asked that I personally email you so I hope you find this email well ~
thank you!

sincerely,

rosie s.

5/12/2011

Dear Professor,

Tomorrow morning i have to work the morning shift at my job i will be in class but i might be like 20 min late. I thought i should let you know in advantage. See you tomorrow for our final class.

best
Rebecca W.

5/13/2011

Dear Professor,

I apologize deeply for not being able to participate in your class as anticipated.
the last few weeks was very hard for me because I was being monitored by a government agency due to my father's due as a diplomat.

I just returned back home safely from Korea and Europe today and I did my best to inform you. I reached out to my cousin rosie to give you an email so I hope you got that.

I did response 3 and 4 during my trip away out the country, so I hope this does best.
I once I again thank you for teaching me many great things in this class in the time that I participated.
I really enjoyed everything and truthfully look at the Guggenheim with such amazement that changed my view in many ways.

Thank you sir,
Leena L.

5/16/2011

Dear Professor,

I would like to apologize for not making it to our last session.
I have been down with the flu for the last few days with a bad
sore throat as well as fever. Really bad timing right at the end
of finals week! :(
I finally felt a little better today and got to finish my project.
I'm attaching my drawing and my text. Not that I'm a great
painter, but I put my feelings into it :)
I want to thank you for a great semester, the course has given
me a lot of good food for thought, and I was exposed to the
issues, dilemmas and matters of another art form that I don't
usually do, and your remarks have been wise and inspiring.
I also thank you for the interest you've shown in my music and
hope to see you at one of my future shows! (I've put you on my
mailing list as you've requested so you'll be notified.)
thank you and have a great summer!

Mendy H.

8/31/2011

Dear Professor,

My name is Mercedez G.-L.and I am a student in your ████████
████ class. Unfortunately, I am not able to attend the first
week of classes because of Hurricane Irene and the cancelation
of my flights to New York. Due to already booked flights this
whole week, I couldn't get on to a flight until this weekend. I
appreciate your understanding and I hope my absence isn't penalized as it was out of my control. Looking forward to meeting you next week, as I am eager and excited to start class.

All the Best,
Mercedez

9/8/2011

Dear Professor,

I have a slightly big problem. I can't get out of my town to get to any highways to get into the city because my town decides to swim every time it rains for 3 days straight. All the bus stops around my town are also closed. Even if I got out now I would have absolutely no way of getting back into my town at 8pm tonight because that when I get home after all my classes. You don't know this but I already missed my first day of classes because I was flooded last week as well. I know it's probably hard to believe but I really live in one of the most flooding areas of NJ but this whole two floods in 2 weeks has never happened before. I know i'm going to have to talk to the Dean because not all of my professors dropped my last absence and if I lower my grade it's because I was slacking not because I didn't have a possible way of getting to class. Therefore I'm so sorry I'm not going to be in class today and I ask you if you could please not count this as an absence. Please let me know if you need any pictures as proof or anything. I'm sure i'll be in class tuesday. This just isn't how I wanted to start my semester.

Peggy L.

9/19/2011

Dear Professor,

My name is Tyson R. I attend your ████████ Tuesday/ Thursday 12:15–1:30 class. I'm sad to inform you that my grandfather had just passed away. Unfortunately I will not be in class Tuesday. I understand that we will be covering some heavy duty topics and I hope that I will be able make up the time and work when I return. I know that I've also been absent once already on Thursday, September 8th due to a play I participated in for the 9/11 memorial events that ████████ held. I have a program as proof that I'll bring in as well as my funeral documents. Thank you for your time Professor.

Tyson R.

9/26/2011

Dear Professor,

I had to be absent on Friday due to the fact that I had to be in the hospital removing stitches from my tonsil removal. However I am doing better and will be visiting the museum before class on Friday so I am able to discuss with the class.

Best,
Leila B.

10/18/2011

Dear Professor,

I have woken up very I'll this morning and will not be able to make it to class. Will you be posting the assignment on back-board? That way I can know when it shall be due and complete it on time. Also, just wanted to let you know that when I return for Thursday's class, I will be ready to present my artist, if you don't have a lecture planned for that day.

Have a good day!

Sincerely,
Louisa R.

10/20/2011

Dear Professor,

i have class with you on tuesdays and thursdays from 12:15 to 1:30, i have missed the last few classes due to severe bronchitis and asthma attacks. under my doctors orders she told me to stay home and recover. i will return to class on tuesday october 25th.i have excuse notes from my doctor so you can verify that i was sick. if you feel the need to call my doctor just let me know and i will give you her office number. i would like to know what assignments i have missed so i can make up the work. also, i would like to know if i have missed any quizzes or tests? thank you and sorry for inconvenience. please email me back at ███@yahoo.com or feel free to call me at 917-███████

Barney B.

11/1/2011

Dear Professor,

This is Mathew H. from your ██████████. I could not make it to class today due to complications at work. This is my paper. I also have the receipt and button from the museum visit that I can bring in thursday.

Mathew H.

11/3/2011

Dear Professor,

This is Lucinda G. from your Tuesday/Thursday classes. I am sorry that I didn't come in on Tuesday I was having Asthma problems that had to be taken care of immmediatley. Here is the paper I was going to bring it in today but I was having some problems in the computer lab that made me unable to print it. So I am just sending it to you, as for the receipt I will had it in to you in class today.

Hope you have a good day
L.G.

11/22/2011

Dear Professor,

Sorry but I won't be able to make it to class I don't feel good. I remember you assigned an essay to exchange characters in the school of Athens painting and you said it was due Thursday but there is no class on Thursday. Please let me know if you want it trough email or if you want a copy the Tuesday we get back from break.

Elvira

11/27/2011

Dear Professor,

its Rusty S. from ur 12:05 – 1:30 class on thursday october 27, 2011 i forgot to sign my name on the attendance and I'm just reminding that i was here today.

11/29/2011

Dear Professor,

Unfortunately I woke up this morning with a horrible stomach virus and won't make it to class today. I'm sorry for another absence and I hope this will not affect my grade for I will definitely make up any work that I've missed. Thank you for your time and understanding.

Tyson R.

1/27/2012

Dear Professor,

I'm so sorry to have missed the first class. I registered moments ago because I realized I had room for it in my schedule. Please let me know if there is anything I can do to prepare for next week.

Thank you,
Joelle C.

2/22/2012

Dear Professor,

I want to apologize for not making it to class last friday, and I would like to know if we are meeting at the Guggenheim next friday, or if it is a normal class.

Thanks,
Paula

2/24/2012

Dear Professor,

I got really bad cold and can't go there today. I am so sorry that i couldn't email you earlier. Could you tell me about the points of today's viewing please?

Thanks,
Yoko N.

3/8/2012

Dear Professor,

I was absent last friday, the second museum outing, because of an emergency, but made it back another day to explore more. I was wondering if there was a response due for tomorrow. Thanks!

Best,
Leah

3/12/2012

Dear Professor,

I would like to apologize for being absent from yesterday's class. I woke up with a fever yesterday morning and was unable to attend any/all of my classes. Attached is my response paper #2. Thank you for understanding and have a pleasant spring vacation.

Sincerely,
Jane D.

3/13/2012

Dear Professor,

This is Argentina from your art class, Im I missed class today.
I come from New Jersey and the trains were delayed today so
I couldn't make it into the city on time. But I shall see you in
class Thursday!

Argentina A.

3/23/2012

Dear Professor,

Just wanted to excuse my absence before spring break, as I did with most of my professors for the classes I missed that week. Sorry I couldn't make your event at The Kitchen, also – I want to go. I figured I'd tell you a little about what's going on with me right now..

For the past few years I have been creating and working on a music project called Dancefloor Diplomacy, and just this past week I debuted its first music video to the public at Anthology Film Archives, and now the internet. It has only been on the internet for a week now, but the press response has been tremendous.

Just to name a few, it was written about by Youtube, The Huffington Post, The L Magazine (mentions my name), Devour, among many others (including Sarah Lawrence – my actual college, I am an exchange student just for this year, and the ███████████'s websites/twitters).

Thus, I went home (to Philadelphia) to do a few interviews, organize a few more press releases, and basically change my spring break plans to accomodate this happening. That said, I am playing major catchup in all of my classes this week for this midterms week. I will be handing in my Guggenheim letter tomorrow, since I know you prefer physical copies.

Check out our video too!
Hope you like it,

Thanks,
JP S.

4/13/2012

Dear Professor,

Unfortunately I will be missing today's class, I am with fever feeling quite bad. I haven't missed a class so far and I'm sad doing so cause I think your classes are wonderful and so interesting full of spontaneity and truth.
Anyways I attach you the assign 3. If you prefer a printed copy let me know and I will print it for next class.

Have a good weekend,
Laura.

4/13/2012

Dear Professor,

Thought I was going to make it into today, but I am still under the weather in bed.
Here is my paper.
Hope you are well.

Best,
JP S.

4/15/2012

Dear Professor,

I just wanted to email you in case I can't make it to class on Tuesday. I just tried to get out of bed and I tripped on my shoe and put all my weight on my left ankle. I hope the picture doesn't gross you out, but you can see it's the size of a golf ball.

Boyd L.

4/28/2012

Dear Professor,

I apologize for my absence today, my roommates were generous enough to pass off their sicknesses on me so I have not been feeling well all day. My apologies again; if i missed anything important could you please fill me in? Thank you very much.

Thanks,
Bradley K.

5/1/2012

Dear Professor,

I don't know what happened, for some reason my email sent out spam. PLEASE don't click anything I send you!

Boyd L.

5/2/2012

Dear Professor,

I cannot attend class this coming Friday, May 4th because I have to go to The Cathedral of St. John the Divine.

I hope this does not mean that I will fail class…

If so, I am willing to do some make up work or an extra response paper.

Let me know what I have to do.

Thank you,
Will H.

5/3/2012

Dear Professor,

I know I am very sorry, I have to go to this Cathedral for a final project.

Is there any make up work I can do for missing class?

I can make class but I might be a little late.

–Will H.

5/3/2012

Dear Professor,

Actually, I will make class because my other obligation starts at ten so that should give me enough time to get over to class by 12 pm

–Will H.

5/9/2012

Dear Professor,

Regarding this week's class (5/11), I will be leaving early because I have a horrible flu and the soonest I could get an appointment with a doctor was at 1 PM on Friday, so I would need to leave around 12:30 PM.

I am hoping to present earlier on in the class or drop my final paper off with you at the beginning of class. If there is another assignment you would like me to do (to make up for my absence,) please let me know and I will gladly do it and submit it on Friday.

I do not mean to disrespect you or your class in any way, and I hope this is alright with you!

Sincerely,
Fiona D.

5/11/2012

Dear Professor,

So sorry for missing the last class today. I was totally tired, and misunderstood that the class was cancelled... because my class on 3–5:40 was actually cancelled today. So sorry about it.

Also, I think I've submitted the first assignment, and the second one but I haven't gotten back both of those...
I was just wondering if you notice that or you did not get them?!

I hope everything is going to be okay because this is my last semester and graduating.
Please let me know if there is any problem on my assignments I can send them to you tomorrow.

Thanks,
Yoko N.

5/29/2012

Dear Professor,

I wanted to let you know that because the course schedule was moved up, I will not be attending the first 2 class sessions. I will be out of town for 2 weeks but I look forward to joining your course upon my return on June 13th. I am really looking forward to your course!

Best,
Madeleine S.

9/5/2012

Dear Professor,

I do not believe I am going to be able to make class today on account of the fact that I need to be home for a repair on my refrigerator. The repairman is late, and I have to be here to let him in. I will try and get notes from someone in the class, but wanted to let you know that I wasn't just skipping. I will see you on Monday. Have a nice weekend.

Max K.

9/5/2012

Dear Professor,

Sorry I missed class today! I overslept and missed two of my classes – is there anything I need to do to make up for it?

Thanks,
Jennifer

9/19/2012

Dear Professor,

I will be missing class the 20th of September. Below is an attached document, proof of the court date.

Ernestine S.

9/24/2012

Dear Professor,

I am very disappointed to have not been physically present in class today. The John Cage and Asia reading was satisfying in resolving a lot of questions I had had, and I like that it implicated Cage as the trickster he was. I was excited to be able to join the discussion with some of my notes. I am unsure of whether or not you find it important, but here is a brief explanation of why I was absent: in May I got into an accident speeding on my skateboard and broke my ankle in two places, tearing an important ligament in that region as well, and I received two surgeries therein. Only recently have I become 100% weight bearing, and though I dislike calling my injury to the attention of professors or using it as an excuse of sorts: at times the pain (which is all in the mind) and swelling become unmanageable. Upon my return, next class, I will provide a doctors note.
Thank you for your time and consideration,

best,
Sandra

9/27/2012

Dear Professor,

I have a conflict on Monday and I need to leave class about thirty minutes early.

This will be the only time that I will have to miss part of class.

Let me know if this is a major issue.

Thanks,
Will H.

10/3/2012

Dear Professor,

Sorry I missed your class this week, but I am getting over a cold finally today, but to make up for it I went to the Guggenheim which puts money in your pocket, so it was not a total loss.

Rex B.

10/17/2012

Dear Professor,

I was going to talk to you on Monday about this, since I wanted to do it in person, but I feel like that might be too much time passed. I've had a combination of being sick and depression wallop me these past weeks and I sincerely apologize for missing so many classes. I would really love to stay in the class, so I was wondering if that was possible. I've kept up with reading and will have my paper on Monday if so. I look forward to hearing from you.

Max K.

10/23/2012

Dear Professor,

i have a doctor's appointment all the way uptown in the morning tomorrow, so might be running a bit late..

Jacob A.

11/5/2012

Dear Professor,

Because of Sandy we are staying with friends out of town and I won't be able to make it back for this evenings' class.
I thought I heard you mention last Friday that there were classes the next two weeks, but in my notes I have class on 11/05 but not on 11/12. The next class after this Monday is on 11/19. Am I correct?

I hope you are doing well as we rebound from this storm.
Herbert L.

11/7/2012

Dear Professor,

I had to make a last minute doc appointment for this morning. I may be able to make it to the second half of class if everything is on time!

Thanks,
Aaron

11/13/2012

Dear Professor,

I just got out of the doctor's office:
they wanted to scar my face and kill what's inside me.
I ran out and did not pay.

Jacob A.

11/14/2012

Dear Professor,

running 10 minutes late, tell everybody I'm coming....thanks!

Vittoria C.

11/14/2012

Dear Professor,

I wanted to share with you that contrary to my wishes i will not be able to give my museum assignment in tomorrow. This unfortunately includes the short presentation as well. I know this message is kind of tardy in itself, but there were a few circumstances that led to its being late.

I'm the student that showed you the hospital letter for the week i missed class. I have chosen a work and have prepared a paper, but it is not quite finalized. I would rather give you something i would be better prepared to speak about. I hope you can give me an extension until Tuesday, i will be ready by then. It would help immensely.

Thank you,

Gregorio C.

11/15/2012

Dear Professor,

im sorry i got caught up in work and missed your class today but i ran to the class and according to the girl who was in there i had just missed you, so i left my essay on the desk hopefully its there on tuesday, if not i will have a copy on me , im just hoping you wont count it as late Thank You

From Geraldine D.

11/19/2012

Dear Professor,

do we have class tomorrow?
sorry about today.. these days i've been part insomniac : sleeping at 6h waking at 13h.
do you want us to write a response to the expo?
i personally found it quite disenchanting and strangely put together..

best,
Jacob A.

11/25/2012

Dear Professor,

i received some really awful news this morning, my best friend who has been battling cancer for the last two years passed away yesterday. i will be in class tomorrow and have completed some of the readings for each of your classes but am finding it very hard to focus and am choosing to spend the day with friends and her family.

thank you for your understanding,

Vittoria C.

11/26/2012

Dear Professor,

I am still in rough shape and not going to be in class today. Thank you for reminding me that everything is music, I know it's true. See you on Wednesday.

Vittoria C.

11/26/2012

Dear Professor,

I have to be on Long Island today for a family emergency. Sorry for the late notice, I will see you Wednesday

Igor

12/5/2012

Dear Professor,

Things on the streets have been really crazy. I have been very distracted watching and listening to what is going on, it is somewhat out of my control. But, I miss you and class. I will be in class on Monday.

Thank you,
Bye
Sandra

12/6/2012

Dear Professor,

No, I am not homeless…but on my way to school and such and over the weekends…yes when i look around on the street …i'll let you know what things, it's a lot…I saw a Buddha in a cage…and a lot of other really crazy things…everyone is smiling at eachother .

It sounds like I'm insane because I have not figured out how to explain it ye,t and I am not using language properly, but everyone I speak to about it has noticed this musical vibration in the street; everyone is dancing; even people I do not know who I have not mentioned feeling anything to , who know I know, are staring at me…literally 95 percent of the people on the street smile at me…like mothers with baby carriages especially…and ghetto people…the whole courtyard at ████████ ██████ is dancing…I keep getting free stuff, so do other people i know…bed-stuy in brooklyn was crazy, that's where I saw the Buddha in the Cage, and I also saw these kids doing an enactment fluxus time performance through a storefront window of the last supper, but with lots of glitter and only three people… and they were blasting this drone from inside their space and it was all through the streets and there was a sign that said "Excercises: come in for tactics" right in front… and there were a bunch of musicians around the store front who stopped and i asked if they feel "it" and they said yes…. Look around, it's pretty interesting what happening behind peoples gazes…like on the train…everyone looks like they're in love, about to cry, or on drugs…

Sandra

12/7/2012

Dear Professor,

Also, other people have said this has come in as useful advice for them...walk away from apples..like if you see someone buying apples at the deli...maybe go to another deli...not out of paranoia, but experimentation...apples are important right now....i.
away from apples towards india...maybe whatever you can gather from that holds some significance in your life too, it's been pretty...helpful in navigating people toward harmonious choices...yea, interesting things have happened.

I'm sure you feel it too. Literally everyone I speak to feels it.

Sandra

12/7/2012

Dear Professor,

I have terrible news. I really tried my best to pass this course but i made the hard decision to try to resign myself from ALL of the courses i signed up for this semsester. It's an appeal prcess. My GPA would have taken a hard hit and I can't afford that as I am trying to transfer to major in Art history.
I enjoyed your class very much, but due to ongoing medical issues I couldn't perform to the best of my abilities.
It really affected me.

Thank you for everything.

Glenda C.

PS I would love to meet one day to inquire about internships with you or any affiliations you may know
I've interned at the ▮▮ Museum so far.

12/11/2012

Dear Professor,

I truly regret having to miss class so much this semester, and I wish that could have been different as I truly enjoyed the experiences that I did have in class. The discussions were lively and thought-provoking. They have to be, I suppose. However, my mental health unfortunately had to take precedent. I am starting weekly therapy this break, and have an appointment on Friday to help once again stabilize the medication that I am on. In any case, I'm writing to you to ask what exactly can be done about my situation. I fully understand if you must fail me. Truthfully, I'm not sure I deserve anything more than that. But, if you believe that my grade could be salvaged with makeup work or anything else, please let me know. I feel like I have failed you as a student, and wish I could take your class next semester to prove that I can actually be a good student who adds to the discourse, but I have a requirement that I need to take at that time. I am not sure if I will see you tomorrow in class, as I am not sure if we are actually meeting, having missed Monday. If we are, we can discuss this further if you'd like. If not, I'll leave you with my seven words.

There's no stability or instability. Only rest.
Max K.

12/12/2012

Dear Professor,

I am so embarrassed by my absences the last few weeks from class. I literally fell off the face of the earth after sandy for almost a month. I just felt like I was dealing with alot with no one in nyc to fall back on and have been incredibly ill the past two weeks on top of it. I know I am going to fail this class and I deserve to for the amount of classes I missed. To be honest, I would be up all night trying to catch up for this and all my other classes before hand and come home from my first class at 8am and then my other one and fall asleep and realize it was too late to come to class when I woke up. I have been reading a lot of Cage however this past few weeks and every time I tried to come back I would be so embarrassed by what I did I just made it worst by putting off reality. I honestly don't deserve anything but if there is any way I can make up some assignments to get at least a satisfactory grade I will do it. I know this email should have been sent much sooner and I should have been in class much more these past few weeks but I literally have been dealing with a lot of stuff like being completely ill and falling back into my depression after sandy and my friend's passing that I just kept making excuses and mistakes for not attending. This is absolutely no excuse at all but I could face expulsion from school and i just found out. Because I have missed a lot of classes this semester in my other classes and got really behind in other aspects that it seems I am in a no win position. My one class I failed for sure but I am working with one of my other teachers to get something that I won't fail. I have also trying to get a note from the disability services to no avail, so I fell into a really bad habit of feeling completely helpless and thinking oh well I can fix it next semester but didn't realize what was gonna happen if I

was gonna fail. I really will do whatever I can to receive the minimum grade to pass. I know this is asking a lot and I don't expect any sympathy for my failure to attend, I just want the opportunity to make things better for both this semester and the opportunity to continue on at school. Please dont think I am trying to guilt you into anything, i totally understand if i am beyond any grade at this point and will work in whatever way i can to continue on at ██████████████ with an appeal to the dean's possible decision. I will accept whatever happens. I can't believe I am sending this email to you because it isn't like me to just throw off my responsibility like i did but my depression had gotten the best of me and I began to think what is the purpose and thought even if I failed I would be able to make up for it but now I see that it could turn out in my expulsion. I am usually really motivated and want to make the best of what I do. I appreciate the time you're taking to read this. I am so sorry about this email and the time it took to send but I was being such a coward. I totally understand whatever you decide about my grade and take full responsibility for all the class that I missed following the storm. Please don't feel obliged in any way to do anything- you don't deserve my faults on your conscious, I thought I would just ask and see if there was any chance at this last minute. Again thanks for your time.
Julian M.

12/13/2012

Dear Professor,

I am terribly sorry to have missed the last class of the semester, unless we will be having class on monday, which I doubt. But I just wanted to say I'm sorry about not being there, but I was at school until two in the morning on Tuesday evening, leaving me extremely exhausted. But there is also good news, I am now an intern at Sperone Westwater on the Bowery!

Sorry again,
Rex B.

2/5/2013

Dear Professor,

I will be out of town and unfortunately not able to attend to-morrow's class. I look forward to meeting with the group on 2/20.

Thank you,
Mabel W.

2/8/2013

Dear Professor,

Emily S. and I are currently upstate and due to the storm we won't be able to make it to class. We will make sure to catch up on everything we missed and will see you next week!

Thank you for understanding,
George

2/8/2013

Dear Professor,

I have been feeling very sick towards the end of this week so I won't be able to make it to class today. Does the school storm warning apply to this class? I will make up anything I miss and see you next week.

Best,
Clarice

2/14/2013

Dear Professor,

I have registered to your class with great enthusiasm but at the end of January I had suffered from shingles which made me unable to attend school. Now I'm completely healed besides a few scars that are left behind and would like to proceed with your class. Since I had a few absences, I wanted to reach out to you and ask if you would accept me "back" into your class.

What I can tell you about me in a "nutshell" is that I am a hard worker, have a great interest in the arts, and take my education very seriously.

Thank you,

Kindest Regards,
Toshiko B.

2/20/2013

Dear Professor,

I hope you're well and see this in time. I'm not sure how regularly you check your email in between teaching and getting traffic tickets. Kidding!
I'm emailing because I will be absent tomorrow, Thursday February 21. There is an information session on a study abroad trip to Italy taking place this summer that I am interested in. The info session is at ██████████ at 12 and that is the only one that I could go to. Just letting you know, because trust me I wouldn't miss your class for something trivial.

Respectfully,
Jeffrey B.

2/27/2013

Dear Professor– I am away for the week and won't be attending the class today. I'm the Caravaggio lover and while I'm not sure if the Met has any, I would be so grateful if you could save any Caravaggio paintings for any future class.

Very much enjoying the lectures.

Thank you,
Michael F.

2/28/2013

Dear Professor,

I am currently sitting in the emergency room with my 8 yr old daughter. We have been here since 11 last night with a fever that shot up to 104.6 and since she suffers from febrile seizures they are keeping her in observation her until all her tests come back.
I had to email you all at once with my phone on low battery indicator.

Carlene H. A.

3/6/2013

Dear Professor,

I would like to confirm that you are having class this Friday. I am not sure if you will have class due to the weather. i would like to make plans to return to Long Island if you think you may cancel. Please let me know. Thank you

christine k.

3/6/2013

Dear Professor,

I wanted to let you know so that the group isn't kept waiting for me that I will be unable to attend this Friday's meeting of ███████████, and will also be unable to come on Friday, March 22.

Love the class!
Claire R.
The short docent from the Met

3/8/2013

Dear Professor,

I'm Yolanda.
The weather! I hate to say this.
Snow has not been cleared yet in my neighborhood, and I do not think it will be any soon. I commute from Long Island.
Sorry. I will try my best to make it on time but if not please be understanding.
Thank you.

Best
Yolanda L.

3/12/2013

Professor– Apologies for the weekly E-mail. I have a meeting in midtown tomorrow at 2:30 pm. I will be heading to your lecture but will probably be late, so if possible to share the itinerary with the group desk at The Met, that would be terrific. This art class is the highlight of my week.

Thanks,
Michael F.

3/19/2013

Dear Professor,

I will be late for 3:15pm's gathering.

I will come up to find you when I arrive later, will you please tell the lady/gentlemen at the desk where you will be heading?

Thank you,
Jeanette J.

3/20/2013

Dear Professor,

I'm sorry I couldn't make it today. I want to catch up. What did I miss today?

Best regards,
Jeanette J.

3/22/2013

Dear Professor,

I will not be able to attend class tomorrow, but I have attached my application letter. I hope class goes well.

Thanks,
Jen

3/22/2013

Dear Professor,

I wanted to apologize for my absence today. I was feeling very ill and was unable to make it. I wanted to send you a copy of my writing assignment for review. Once again, I apologize and hope you have a wonderful spring break.

Best Regards,

Ida R.

4/5/2013

Dear Professor,

I am very sorry but I misread the syllabus and did not see your email yesterday about our museum visit so I arrived at class a little while ago and then no one was there and then realized the mistake I made! I was wondering if it would be possible for me to go visit the museum myself and see the exhibit we are supposed to see and do an extra credit assignment, just because I do not have anyones number from the class and with timing will not be able to make it there for a while and will miss most of the class. I am very sorry about this!

Sincerely,
Farah

4/19/2013

Dear Professor,

I'm very sorry, but I overslept and then when I tried to drop off my paper at class at 1:51 you were already gone.
So, I have attached my paper. I hope you like it and I'm very sorry I missed class.

Regads,
Jen

4/24/2013

Dear Professor,

Please don't wait for me this Friday afternoon, as unfortunately I have a doctor's appointment. I would rather be looking at art.

Will be with you all for the last class next week.

Best regards,
Claire R.

4/26/2013

Dear Professor,

I'm really sorry but I don't think I can make it to class today. I've had a bad cold all week and this cough seems to have gone into my lungs (?!). I'm planning on going into the clinic later today. Hopefully it's nothing serious.

I hope you guys have a good museum visit. See you next week,

Amanda

5/17/2013

Dear Professor,

I hope you are doing fine and in the best of health. A case is pending against me since 2010 and now I have been reprimanded in ▮▮▮ County Correctional Center.

I miss attending class and I have learned to appreciate and better understand the work of artists from the renaissance. Tintoretto, as a humble painter, have opened the humanist window for me through his paintings as he closed the doors to Italian Renaissance Art.

Thanks for teaching us how to investigate artwork. How to see not just the micro and macro, but the areas of the painting, drawing or sculpture that are not visible to the eyes but to the mind. Art through humanism by humanist for humans with regards to God.

Sincerely,
Russel D.

P.S. Remember to stop for the traffic light.

6/5/2013

Dear Professor,

I woke up not feeling well this morning, so may not be able to come to class today. I am so very sorry.

If you have a moment, could you tell me what galleries/artists you will be covering today so that I can go there on my own?

Also, I would be grateful to know what you would like us to read.

Very Sincerely,
Beverly M.

6/7/2013

Dear Professor,

Sorry to have missed class on Thursday. I was ill.
Were there any reading asignments?

Thanks,
Joyce C.

6/12/2013

Dear Professor,

I am so dreadfully sorry but I came down with a bad virus yesterday, and so again, sadly, I am going to need to again miss your class. (Last week's "episode" ended in a rather scary nose bleed and I ended up at my internist's office!)

I "googled" you and find you and your work totally fascinating and intriguing.

I had been thinking of writing you to learn more about your approach in this particular class and then decided, because I became so interested in your work, that I would just go today and find out myself!

I would so much like to know the kind of approach you are taking in this particular course, which reads in the description like a selective "survey" of art history (if such a thing is really possible!) from the Early Renaissance to the 20th Century, but my sense from you very kind letter last week, your course is more interesting than that

And I feel almost "embarrassed" to say that what I was thinking about, when I signed up, was to do an art history course, that would be a more chronological and "traditional" in approach.

Many years ago, I majored in art history and did some graduate study, primarily from a rather purely "formalist" perspective, which definitely had it strong limitations.

And I am writing with total respect from my sense of you and your work.

I am thinking that I may be taking some vacation time in July, so am thinking that I would probably end up missing at least another class meeting.

If it seems that maybe I should take another course with you at another time since I am already missing two classes, I would be so grateful to know what and when you will be teaching in the fall or any other time. If you teach at another school, I would also be very pleased in knowing this.

With my best wishes,

Beverly M.

6/13/2013

Dear Professor,

I am so glad that you will be doing more classes and at a variety of places.

And it is also great to know that you will be teaching this same class in the fall.

I haven't withdrawn from the class as yet, and I am tempted to come as best I can, and then maybe also repeat it in the fall.

I would imagine that the class would be a bit different each semester, perhaps covering different artists?

Sometimes I can be a bit "shy" about class participation and wonder what your thoughts are about this.

Do you feel that it is possible to get enough out of the class if one comes without doing a great deal of reading because my schedule may be a bit tight in the coming weeks?

I truly hope that you do not mind my asking all of these questions!

With my good wishes,

Beverly M.

6/13/2013

Dear Professor,

I hope to be able to join in next week!!

I am in the final "throes" of preparing for a chorus concert at the 92nd Street Y, a community chorus dedicated to the American musical theater and also film sometimes, so I have been feeling a bit stressed out!! Fortunately, for me, there are no solos!!!

More soon, Best from

Beverly M.

6/13/2013

Dear Professor,

Unfortunately, I will not be able to make it to class this afternoon...but, I will look forward to seeing you next week. In the meantime, here's a question that I'm pondering:

If an artist has his work done by those in his studio or atelier, can it really be said to be his work? Is he really "there"? I am thinking specifically of the review of Damien Hirst's work (Hirst, Globally Dotting His 'I') but, the same can be said for any of the artists who did the same.

Have a good week!

Deborah

6/19/2013

Dear Professor,

As much as I am looking forward to studying with you, I made the hard decision of waiting until the fall semester to take your class.

Since I missed two classes already, and expect to be traveling a bit in the latter part of July, I am afraid that I would be missing at least one other class.

I am sorry that I will have to wait until the fall to study with you, but will plan to read your book before class starts.

I want to wish you an excellent summer and I truly appreciate our e-mails.

With my best wishes,

Beverly M.

10/9/2013

Dear Professor,

I apologize for not contacting you sooner. My name is Celestine H. and I am in your Wednesday classes from (2–5). I tore my ligament last week in a gymnastics class at Chelsea piers and I am still recovering. I have been on bedrest and was not able to walk, I am getting better. I thought I would be able to make it to class today but unfortunately my leg still hurts. I haven't been able to make it to the MET either. I would hate to see this injury affect my grade. Is their any assignment I can do in compensation, or an extension? Please contact me as soon as you can. I really do not want my grade harmed and I'm willing to do extra in light of the work I missed.

Thank you,
Celestine H.

10/21/2013

Dear Professor,

Last Friday's ███████████ was delightful – and it was nice seeing ███████████ again.

Unfortunately I won't be able to attend any more of the ███████
███ groups.
I have a fractured knee-cap!

After we parted on 57th Street I went to Bergdorf Goodman to do a little shopping – (looking – not buying – it's a bit too expensive, but fun to look).

At about 6:45 I walked back to 6th Avenue to take to F train home. While crossing 57th Street I somehow or other tripped right in the middle of the street (it was already dark, but I think it may have been on a manhole cover). I landed smack down on my left knee!!! Luckily a nice young man walking behind me helped me up and got me to the curb – then a couple who saw the whole thing got me a taxi. It was a miracle that we didn't get hit by any cars turning onto 57th St from 6th Ave. Bill met me at the ER at Beth Israel Hospital – I was X-rayed – diagnosis – fractured patella.

We just came back from seeing my orthopedist who is a knee and hip specialist to have everything rechecked. I'm in the lucky 20% that doesn't have to have surgery. But, I have to be in an air-splint to keep my knee immobile for 4 – 6 weeks. It still hurts and I'm walking with crutches – not fun! And then there will be lots of Physical Therapy. C'est la vie!

So there goes the rest of the ███████████.

Hopefully I'll see you in the spring.

Enjoy the rest of the sessions – enjoy the holidays – and stay well.

Yours,

Sally

10/23/2013

Dear Professor,

I am writing to let you know that I will be unable to attend class because of a few things that are going on. I would rather not discuss in email but will am willing to speak to you about it when I come to next weeks class the problem is pretty sensitive to me. I will follow the reading as I am supposed to and just wanted to give you a heads up on missing the class. Thank you very much

Shawn Reed

11/6/2013

Dear Professor,

I'm on all kinds of meds and I can't even think, as evident by my women's history "knowledge". I know you don't read all your emails but I want this to serve as evidence of communication.

Thank you and have a good rest of the week!

Do not print this email unless absolutely necessary.

Blanca G.

12/2/2013

Dear Professor,

Hope you're well.

I just wanted to give you a heads up/make sure it's ok that I will not be in class this Friday...

As you know, my job as a research assistant for the Gordon Matta-Clark project doesn't normally intersect with my school schedule but this week (of all weeks!) there was no way around this Friday, and I have to travel upstate to interview some wack job.

Let me know your thoughts and if there's anything I can do to keep up for Friday. I am deeply disappointed about missing one of our last classes.

Fondly,
Nadine T.

12/4/2013

Dear Professor,

I am extremely sick and will not be able to attend our art class for today, Wednesday, December 4th. Would you like for me to email you my essays or bring them in next session?

Kendall U.

12/12/2013

Dear Professor,

Please see attached my proposal for the artist for the "new museum" in the 21st century.

Unfortunately, I am flying back to China tomorrow and won't be able attend the discussion tomorrow. I wish you a great holiday! Please let me know if you have any questions regarding view the attached file.

Thank you very much,

Best,

Reiko

12/18/2013

Dear Professor,

here are my police report copy and hospital paper from what we spoke about in last weeks class I tried to get them printed out but was unable to so I send it in the email. Thank you for your understanding and patience.

Shayne R.

1/31/2014

Dear Professor,

I think I missed class this week by a hair, I showed up around 12:25 and the room was empty. I still want really would like to take the class, let me know what I can do to get started on the right foot.

Sincerely

Clark S.

2/5/2014

Dear Professor,

I am so sorry, but, because of the weather, I will not be able to attend the first meeting of ████████████. I live in Connecticut; there does not seem to be any reasonably safe way to get from where I live to the train station. I do plan to attend all of the remaining classes.

Edith M.

2/7/2014

Dear Professor,

I'm really sorry this isn't exactly "advance notice," but I woke up with pink eye this morning, and unfortunately I can't really open my eyes enough to leave the house today.

Is there anything I can do to learn what I've missed at the meeting?

Edith M.

2/13/2014

Dear Professor,

I am a student in your Thursday 2:50pm ████████ class.
I won't be in class today due to the terrible commute from the
North Bronx.

Thanks,
Briana B.

2/25/2014

Dear Professor,

Sorry for not being able to attend class today but my grand-mother fractured her hips and had to take her to the Emergency room. I'm very sorry and will be attending class regularly after today.

Nathan V.

3/5/2014

Dear Professor,

I cannot make todays scheduled event due to a scheduling conflict that I did not previously consider. Can I do the following piece instead?

Julia R.

3/20/2014

Dear Professor,

I understand that the MoMA Assignment was originally due on March 13th, and I apologize for the lateness. However, I was not in school last Thursday, nor today. I understand that there is no excuse for handing in an assignment this late, but I do hope that you accept it.

Attached to this email is my essay for the painting of my choice. I will be bringing a hard copy to class when I go in, but I hope that this is efficient for now.

Again, I apologize for not handing this assignment in on time.

Thank you,
Dorothea R.

3/26/2014

Dear Professor,

I wanted to let you know that I cannot attend class tomorrow. I have caught a rather nasty stomach virus and I can barely stand.

See you next week,
Zane L.

3/28/2014

Dear Professor,

I've been traveling and have not been able to attend the ████████████ classes until today. I just wanted to make sure that today's class is as it appears on the schedule and that there has not been a change.

Thank you,

Traci S.

4/9/2014

Dear Professor,

I apologize for missing class on April 8th, 2014 I was attending a ████████████ sponsored conference. I will be in attendance tomorrow, i have attached a letter from ███ explaining my absence. My apologies on my missing assignments i have been on light duty after receiving an on the job injury.

Enjoy your day,
Owen Q.

4/22/2014

Dear Professor,

I am sorry that I did not get to class on time to take the final, due to family emergency. If possible may I still be able to take it.

Kathey W.

4/24/2014

Dear Professor,

I cannot make it to class today I am quite sick. I understand we have an assignment to hand in and I will email it to you if that is ok. Also I will bring in a copy of it next class.

Thank You,
Zane L.

4/24/2014

Dear Professor,

I wasn't feeling well so I could not make it to class today. I have my third assignment to hand in. Would you like me to email it to you, or should I hand in a hard copy next week along with the fourth assignment? Thanks! Have a good weekend!

Natalia P.

5/7/2014

Dear Professor,

It was so nice meeting you a couple of weeks ago; so great to put a face with the name!

I am emailing you to let you know that I am planning on putting up all my event posts by Friday evening! I spoke to you last time about my medical issues and unfortunately I've been in and out of hospital rooms since we last spoke...luckily though I made it to a few events before that so I just need to look through my notes I took and write up my posts.

I will not be able to make the ballet tonight (which I am so upset about) as I am doing some testing this afternoon that will likely require lots of morphine afterwards...the good news is that my friend dances for the ballet and is going to give me a little tour and performance tomorrow morning!

Thank you and I'll be in touch,

Ali L.

5/29/2014

Dear Professor,

I have registered for your ███████████ starting June 4th and very much look forward to these sessions. Unfortunately two weeks ago while in the Sahara desert I fell off a camel and fractured 4 ribs. I am in Paris recuperating but as you probably know only time and pain killers are the treatment. I will not be able to travel in time to make the first session on 4th June but hope to be in New York in time for the second and subsequent sessions.
I would appreciate your input on the following:
– venue as to where to meet at 3:15pm stating on June 11th
– should I obtain any reading or other materials needed or desirable for the course
– would you have an outline or any notes you could let me have on the material you will cover (and I will miss) for the first session.
I look forward to meeting with you.

kind regards
Paul C.

7/11/2014

Dear Professor,

I will not be at the next 2 sessions. A loss since I found the sessions to be very interesting. Please e-mail when your next class will be.

Thanks,

Beth S.

7/24/2014

Dear Professor,

I was very sorry I had to miss your last class on the 20th Century. The 6 classes I attended were excellent. Your choice of art and your highly interesting discussion was really very thought provoking which I greatly enjoyed. I do hope to catch up with you again.

kind regards
Paul C.

9/3/2014

Dear Professor,

I hope you had a great summer.

I am unable to attend our class meeting on Monday September 8th as I will be out of town – I am shooting a dance film with a friend in Long Island. Would it be possible for me to select my events and send them to you, as I did last semester? Let me know if this is okay.

Looking forward to taking the class again!

Thanks,
Sarah

9/11/2014

Dear Professor,

My name is Kiersten B. I recently registered for your class. I switched one of my classes for yours. Anyway, I am sorry for my absence. I misread the schedule and thought it was for another time. I hope I can be excused this one time for your class. Is there a syllabus online? I look forward to your █████ █████. Thanks.

Kiersten B.

9/30/2014

Dear Professor,

I apologize for missing class this past Friday, I was under the sincere impression that class was canceled due to the jewish holiday, as it was Wednesday and Thursday. I am upset with myself for missing class because it has been so enjoyable. If there is anything I can do to make up the time I missed please let me know. Thanks for your time and consideration.

Best regards,
David G.

10/17/2014

Dear Professor,

I am writing to you in regards to the two missing responses I have for Rock Bottom and Midnight Moment. For the past month I have been grieving a death of a very close friend of mine, as well as dealing with very hard family situations. I have been missing a lot of class and going to therapy, and finally able to catch up on work. I understand the structure of this class is to go to the shows, then within the week respond to the questions we provide, but I was curious if there was any way I could still send in my responses? I understand any point deductions that would have to be made.

I would like to maintain a good grade in this course because I am actually really excited and appreciative of all the different art forms we have the opportunity to witness! Please let me know what I can do, and if there is any possible extra credit as well.

Thank you and have a good weekend,
Trevor K.

10/20/2014

Dear Professor,

I didn't want to speak to anyone about this, but I've been urged to contact the school about a personal emergency. I originally sent my adviser an email because I didn't know who I was supposed to notify about this. He has yet to respond to me, and so I've decided to contact my professors directly. I probably should've done this sooner, but it just wasn't on my mind.

I got a phone call on Thursday morning that ████████████ ████ was comatose in ICU from an overdose and I was asked to ████████████. I did just that and I didn't even think to email anyone until I knew what was going on. ████████████ ████████████████████████████ passed away on Saturday morning. I've been paralyzed. I don't really know how to react to this. We are burying him tomorrow morning.

I understand that this isn't what I'm supposed to be thinking about right now, but I know that soon I will be worrying about my academic performance. I have to be honest, I haven't done any school work since Thursday and I was planning on completing my responses and attending the Decolonized Skies exhibit during this week. Anyway, I'm not sure what's supposed to come of this. I'm kind of lost. It seemed like a good idea to contact my professors considering that I've received no response from anyone else. Thanks.

– Tara R.

10/21/2014

Dear Professor,

It's Clinton F. from ████████. I'm sorry I missed class today, and have to miss class Thursday as well. I had to travel to Miami for personal reasons. I will make up any work I miss. Is there anything due on Thursday that I need to hand in? Again I'm sorry for missing out. Hope all is well.

Clinton F.

10/29/2014

Dear Professor,

I apologize for missing class last friday 10/24, I did'nt notice the email you had sent out about class not meeting at the gallery until I got there and was looking around for the class. In lieu of my absence I traveled to the Philadelphia Museum of Art for the first time and enjoyed a few replications of Duchamp's work. I will see you at the gallery this Friday 10/31 unless otherwise notified.

Best,

David G.

10/30/2014

Dear Professor,

This is Esperanza B. from your ▮▮ class on Thursdays at 2:50. I'm sorry for being absent today, I live in Staten Island and they were doing work on the tracks and by the time I would've got to class, it would've pretty much been over. Can I please e-mail you my paper? I have a doctor's appointment next week.

Esperanza B.

10/31/2014

Dear Professor,

I have been out the past few classes due to an infection.

I am on antibiotics and should be able to come back to class.

I am sorry for missing the past couple classes and I wanted to know if I could make up anything?

Anyways I will be in class soon.

Thank you,
Will H.

11/1/2014

Dear Professor,

Unfortunately, something unexpected came up and I will be unable to attend tonights show. I'm so sorry for the inconvenience. Is there a way I would be able to get a ticket to the either of the other dance shows?

Hope all is well

Thank you
Sam Z.

11/7/2014

Dear Professor,

I will not be in class today, I have to go back home to Massachusetts this weekend. Please let me know if there is anything I need to make up.

Thanks,
Suzy

11/7/2014

Dear Professor,

Cataract surgery on Monday was uneventful, just as everyone said.

However …… I still can't see clearly out of that eye – it's like I'm looking through a piece of white gauze (or a dirty milk bottle). The doctor said it's an inflammation under the cornea and that it will improve daily. I've been putting in all my drops and it has improved. However, I still can't see clearly. At the rate it's going I don't think it will be that much better by to-morrow afternoon.

So – have a good week, and hopefully I'll see you at Gagosian next Friday.

Yours,
Sally

11/10/2014

Dear Professor,

sorry not to get in touch with you sooner... the past four weeks have been hectic, i fractured my ankle and was out of town for a week due to a relatives passing. needless to say I AM VERY BEHIND ON WORK. regretfully, i missed out on the pina bauch performance... would it be possible to join the Jaro event? if i have to pay for my ticket, i am okay with that. i will be sending you my responses soon!

best,
Bianca M.

11/14/2014

Dear Professor,

I've just been informed that I need to make the trip to Connecticut today at 3pm for my long waited MRI scan. I won't be able to attend the show unfortunately and don't want the ticket going to waste :(I hope you enjoy the show and please let me know what I can do to fulfill the requirement in another way?

Trevor K.

11/14/2014

Dear Professor,

I am SO SORRY I missed the show tonight, I have the flu so I've been sleeping all day but I thought I was going to make it. I feel so terrible! I know the tickets are very pricey, perhaps I could reimburse you for my ticket?

Again, I am so, SO sorry!

Please let me know what I can do…
Bea C.

11/15/2014

Dear Professor,

I am scheduled to go to the Julliard dance event on Monday. But most Unfortunitly my grandmother passed away on Thursday. The funeral service is Monday so I will not be able to attend the event. I hope you are able to give someone else my ticket.

Please let me know of there is any way fore
To make this up.

Thank you.
Virginia G.

11/21/2014

Dear Professor,

Unfortunately I don't think I'll be able to attend the last class.
Monday's surgery (all 15 minutes of it) on the second eye went well and it's healing nicely – first eye is doing much better. They still need to learn how to work together!
There's a lot of glare – bright light is unpleasant (the computer is killing me) – lots of squinting. Viewing art doesn't seem to be a great idea right now!!!

Hope to see you in March.
Happy Holidays!
Sally

12/9/2014

Dear Professor,

I wanted to notify all of you that I just now got out of the hospital, but still recovering. I am also still out of state and don't know when I'll be back in New York. I would still like to finish out the semester and I was wondering where to go from here. If there are any finals I can make up via email, please let me know when I need to send them in.

Thank You,
Meghan. B.

12/9/2014

Dear Professor,

Attached please find my new readymades and Duchamp diary.

Unfortunately I will be out of town on our last day doing music but I will be channeling this class along the way.

Here are the final assignments,

I'll see you next semester, have a great holiday!

Will H.

12/10/2014

Dear Professor,

I should have contacted you sooner but I've been something of a mess lately. I apologize for being so late-minute, it's unfair to you.

I don't mean to get too personal and I regret having to play the pity card, but since ██████ passing, ████████ has been irrationally clinging to me in a deeply unhealthy way and I've been regularly coerced – and sometimes threatened – by ██ ██████ to commute back to ████████████████████ ██████ to be with ██. This happens every Thursday night into every Monday morning and sometimes even during the week. I've lost my job because of this. But more importantly, it has made it very hard for me to do my school work – ████████ ██ is not a positive aspect of my life in general and so I can't get anything done while I'm at home.

Sob story aside, I'm worried that I will fail your course. I'm already disappointed that I haven't been able to fully enjoy it this semester (it was something that I looked forward to when I signed up for it in the spring). I wanted to ask you if there is any possible way I could receive an acceptable grade at this point. It's entirely understandable if that's not possible, I expected as much. ███████████████████████████ has made it so that if this is the case, I will be allowed to withdraw without penalty due to my extenuating circumstances.

But, if it's at all possible that I can still earn an okay grade, and if you'd be open to giving me an incomplete for them semester and allowing me to finish my work in a timely manner, I would much rather take that route because, 1) having a W on my transcript looks dreadful to prospective grad schools and, 2) I actually went to these events and loved the experience of them, and I feel terrible about not being able to complete my work for this class.

Please let me know what you think. Thank you so much for suffering through this long-winded and long-overdue email.

–Tara R.

1/27/2015

Dear Professor,

this is Alicia H. I registered for this course for the spring term.
I just would like to inform you I won't be there for the first
class, however
I would like to see if possible the syllabus, and any content I
will miss from the first class.

Alicia H.

2/5/2015

Dear Professor – there's a chance I'll have to miss class tomorrow. I'm moving out of my parents' house to williamsburg, and i don't know exactly when it's happening tomorrow. it depends on the movers.

i'll email you again tomorrow if i cant come. maybe we could meet midweek to talk about what happens in class tomorrow?

Jeffrey S.

2/17/2015

Dear Professor,

I am really sick and will not be able to attend class today.

Sincerely,
Melanie D.

2/17/2015

Dear Professor,

Sorry will not be able to attend your class was hit by SUV and have foot and leg injuries.

Hope see you in summer.

Regards,
Beth S.

2/23/2015

Dear Professor,

I am so sorry but I just found out I have to work on Wednesday from 2–6 pm...it's a Principals Conference. So, I will not be able to attend class this week, which is definitely my loss. I will look forward to seeing you a week from Wednesday!

Best,
Deborah

2/24/2015

Dear Professor,

I am in your ████████████ class and I was feeling under the weather today so I did not attend class. I just wanted to let you know about my absence.

Allegra M.

2/26/2015

Dear Professor,

Unfortunately I will not be able to attend today – Will be there next week

April P.

2/27/2015

Dear Professor,

I am looking forward to the course. I will, however, be out of town on the 6th of March until March 25 th. It was already a planned trip. So I just wanted to let you know and will be in NY all the rest of the visits.

Thank you Dr. Ronald L.

2/27/2015

Dear Professor,

I am not going to be able to attend today's class at the Echoes exhibition due to illness. I will be sure to view the works online and go to the gallery another time on my own if possible.

Thank you,
Charlotte H.

2/27/2015

Dear Professor,

I'm really sorry I wasn't able to join you guys at the Guggenheim recently, there was a very unexpected death of a close family member to me. However things are much less hectic now and I'll be able to join you all in NoHo today.

I just wanted to inform you of what has been going on, and thank you in advance!

Christine O.

3/2/2015

Dear Professor,

Because I wasn't in class last Friday, I was wondering if you spoke at all about any assignments for class this week. Is the essay due March 6 on the assignments sheet still applicable? Please let me know.

Thank you,
Charlotte H.

3/4/2015

Dear Professor,

I am one of your students, ███████████'s course and I missed the first class, do we meet at the Midtown Center tomorrow for our second class or we meet at the Metropolitan?

Thank you very much,
Sonia G.

3/5/2015

Dear Professor

I had missed last class and arrived to class today to realize that today is the field trip. I was wondering if it were possible that I can go to MoMa on my own>?

Also about the paper can it be any type of artwork or is there anything specific you want us to see??

Thank You
Best Regards
Annie V.

3/5/2015

Dear Professor,

I apologize for not being able to make it to class today, but I did not want to risk getting stuck in the city during the snowstorm. I live on Long Island and the trains tend to get canceled when the weather is bad outside. I was also sick last Thursday. Are the museum assignments due next Tuesday?

Nanette P.

3/5/2015

Dear Professor,

Is there any chance that today's class can be rescheduled due to the weather?

I am reluctant to come down town (I am in Riverdale, the Bronx), only to find out that the class has been cancelled.

Would appreciate a response. Btw, I tried calling the school but had no response.

Cecile S.

P. S. I so enjoyed your class last week. I was totally engrossed and transported to a different dimension. That's no easy for me with my hectic life. Thank you.

3/6/2015

Dear Professor,

Unfortunately, I was unable to attend class this afternoon due to my problems with diabetes. I was really looking forward to the trip today and hope to see you next week to find what I missed. Do let me know if there is anything I need to prepare for that class.

Best regards,
Ahmed A.

3/6/2015

Dear Professor,

Hope all is well. As I mentioned to you last class I am unable to attend class today because I am helping out this weekend at an art fair. I am very sorry for the inconvenience and hope its not a. Anyways, attached is the essay due for today. I hope it is not a problem that I email it to you. If it is please let me know and I can bring a print version for next class. I am sorry for inconvenience. Thank you.

Best
Simone W.

3/10/2015

Dear Professor,

this is Lola R. (from you tuesday/thursday class at 12:15 am).
Although i was unable to make it to your class here is the museum assignment that is due. If you would like me to make you a hard copy by the next class just let me know. Enjoy the rest of your day.

Lola R.

3/10/2015

Dear Professor,

This is Precious M. S. your student from ███████████. I did not attent class today because I have a job interview. I completed the assignment showing below.

Thanks and have a nice day.

Precious M. S.

3/13/2015

Dear Professor,

Unfortunately I can't make it to class today. Where is your mail box at school so that I can drop off the paper?!

Helene P.

3/13/2015

Dear Professor,

I was feeling horrible today, but I wanted to send you my paper. I can bring a print out next class if that's easier. Here ya go!

See you next week,
Arthur K.

3/18/2015

Dear Professor,

I'm going to be absent this Friday, I have not had a vacation in so long and have been invited out to montauk Thursday evening. I know this is my third absence, and I promise there will be no more!! Hoping this is alright with you given I don't miss anymore classes.

All the best,
Arthur K.

3/18/2015

Dear Professor,

I regret that I will not be at today's meeting. I spent a sleepless night and feel too tired and lacking the energy I need to make the trip to the museum.

Best,
Louise F.

3/23/2015

Dear Professor,

According to the syllabus we are scheduled to visit the MET tomorrow and since I missed Thursdays class I just wanted to make sure. Thank you

Craig S.

4/2/2015

Dear Professor,

I am sick and not able to make it to class. Thank you,

Craig S.

4/2/2015

Dear Professor,

I was unable to attend class today because my boyfriend and I
got evicted and had to find a temporary place to stay.
I was wondering if I could email you my paper since I forgot to
bring it in or if I could bring it to you next class?
Sorry for the inconvenience.

From,
Nyla G.

4/3/2015

Dear Professor,

Apologies for no doubt misspelling your name!
I am so sorry that I missed the last class and I wanted to let you know what a pleasure the class was and how wonderful to learn from you
I already loved Vermeer but now I feel as though I have an enhanced appreciation.
I am hoping to take your next class so hopefully I will see you soon

Best regards.
Jane

4/3/2015

Dear Professor,

I made a HUGE planning error and I can't come to class today. I don't think I told you about my cupcake company – but we're catering an event at ps1 tonight and if I come to class we will not be even close to ready!! The invite is attached, as is my paper that I owe you (I know you want a hard copy and I can leave it in your box on Monday if that's better for you – SO SORRY this is so late I feel like I'm really fucking up – will do anything you want me to to catch up)

Anyway. We're called ████, and if you wanna check us out we're on Instagram @████████ and ████.tumblr.com

Jeffrey S.

4/9/2015

Dear Professor,

I'm writing to notify you that I may not be in class tomorrow. I'm currently working on a documentary as a voiceover artist but I must be in the recording studio tomorrow from 11–1pm. I will try to come in to class if I finish early enough so I don't miss too much, but I didn't want to leave you in the dark. Is there anything I should know that will be discussed in class tomorrow?

Again, I'm sorry for the last minute notice
Jonah C.

4/14/2015

Dear Professor,

I am unable to go to class today because I am feeling under the weather. I wanted to let you know and I hope to be back in class on Thursday. I hope this absence dies not affect my grade too much. Thank you for your time.

Allegra M.

4/15/2015

Dear Professor,

my name is Corinne M. i am in your art class and recently missed class and the assignment. The reason for this is that i have been in and out of the hospital because my grandmother was sick and died yesterday morning. I have not been able to work or deal with my current class requirements and hope i still have the chance to do so. If there is a chance i can still make the work up it will be greatly appreciated. I do have all documents and proof incase its needed. Sorry for the inconvenience.

Sincerely,
Corinne M.

4/17/2015

Dear Professor,

I'm sorry I was unable to be in class today…honestly, I have still been having a bit of trouble getting back to normalcy after the recent events in my life; I have had a lot of trouble getting to sleep, and so I've also had an equally hard time waking up in the morning. This being said, I was down for the count this morning. I'm sorry to be getting it to you so late, but my paper is attached below. I hope you can understand…I'm working every day to feel a little more normal and for my life to be a little more organized. By next Friday, I'm hoping I'll have it together, and I look forward to our class. Enjoy your weekend!

Best,
Yasmin M.

4/18/2015

Dear Professor,

I have to miss class this Friday to go on a field trip for a different class, there have been a few options to attend different field trips, but they all have been scheduled for Friday mid day. The professor is more than happy to send you an email if necessary, let me know. I wish they could've chosen another day! I have the class tomorrow and will inquire about the possibility of me doing one of these trips on my own time so that I don't have to miss your class (honestly I'd rather go to your class), but I'm not sure what the situation with that is because the trip is supposed to be led by someone who knows what to say/ where to go.

All the best,
Arthur

4/21/2015

Dear Professor,

I wanted to know if I can still pass your class even though I have a few absences. If there is a problem because I have been absent please let me know. I have valid reasons for missing 2 days in a row. I hope that you can let me know soon. If you need proof of why I was absent last week I can give you a note signed by my psychologist. Thank you for your time.

Allegra M.

4/23/2015

Dear Professor,

I did not attend Tuesday s class due to the passing of my grandfather. 4/21/15

Craig S.

4/23/2015

Dear Professor,

I wanted to remind you that I will be on military orders from May 1–16. I will be in class next week on April 28 to discuss options regarding the final exam. I appreciate your attention to the matter at hand. If you need to get in touch with me, please feel free to email me or call my cell phone. I have also attached a copy of my orders from the base.

Thank you,

Eduardo P.

Cell–(917) ▮▮▮▮▮▮▮

4/26/2015

Dear Professor,

I have attached the letter from my therapist who I see every week because I have had some issues that have effected me. In the letter it does not say I was with my therapist during the days I was absent last week but that I am suffering from depression. Last week 4/14 & 4/16 I felt too overwhelmed with sadness and depression to attend class. I do believe I can continue the class till the end but if this letter is not enough for me to continue your class I understand. Thank you for your time.

Allegra M.

5/5/2015

Dear Professor,

I am unable to attend class today because Sunday early morning I was stabbed downtown. I did not think to get a doctor's note when I was in the E.R so I have uploaded the diagnosis sheet, as well as a picture of my pants. I would send you a picture of the laceration but I think that would be TMI. I've been told to rest my leg for a few days and to not do too much movement. I am hoping I will be able to walk by Wednesday. I have also attached my exhibition review.

Best,
Drew S.

5/12/2015

Dear Professor,

In case you wouldn't have guessed from my email,
It's Clinton F. from ██████████.

I am emailing you because I recognize that I have been absent quite frequently, but I would like to explain that it is because I have had a severe case of Bronchitis this semester. As I explained most days I saw you, it has hindered my capacity to make it to class on those days that I missed. I have looked into the work we were to discuss, and I've stayed up to date on the work. I hope you understand, and I'm sorry for missing classes as often as I have.

Clinton F.

5/14/2015

Dear Professor,

Unfortunately I have a lease signing in Brooklyn tomorrow at 1:30pm and I realized this is during our class time, however this is the only time available with my landlord.

I wanted to ask you about assignments for this semester, as I still need to send you the final paper and gallery review. Is there a time I can stop by your office to submit these to you or would you prefer that I email them?

Thanks for a great semester, this course has been amazing and I'm so glad I was able to experience it!

Have a good summer!
Jonah C.

4/18/2015

Dear Professor,

I am very sorry about the lateness of my assignments. And my absences during the semester. I am graduating after this semester and I found myself swamped with a ton of work I was not expecting. All of this piled up with vet visits, caring for my new puppy, and other things getting in the way I lost a lot of my energy this semester. I've attached all the assignments in this email. And if there is anything else I can give you please let me know.

Thank you for a great semester and for understanding,

All the best,
William

5/27/2015

Dear Professor, thought you like this photo.

Actually the real reason I'm getting in touch. I fell about 10 days ago and really banged up my back. My physical therapist doesn't see that I can take the Met course. It just kills me. I hope I can join one class towards the end that would be great.

Have a great summer,
Sylvia

6/25/2015

Dear Professor,

My knee and ankle have been more inflamed this week so I'l
have to rest and ice them all day. Sorry to miss the art gallery
class!
Should be there next week.
Have a good weekend.

Best
Grace F.

7/4/2015

Dear Professor,

I had to miss last class, which is very sad to me since you promised to talk about Rembrandt, to look at Rembrandt. There was an exhibition of "self portraits" of Rembrandt in London last January, I was lucky to be there to see the portraits... I was foolish to think that it's me going to see portraits of Rembrandt and ask him questions, all the way around. It was him looking at me and asking me questions...

Not long time ago, I thought of Rembrandt and Dostoevsky – not the first one to compare actually, to the deepest parts of human soul. Who else can do it... Rembrandt did it, I went to see his works and as an echo I saw him asking me questions... I didn't have an answer, still don't. I'd rather to have a mask to tell the truth.

What is the rarest gift I thought, attention as you said or to be the humanist as I only start to learn. I would say it is the rarest gift today for all of us.

To tell you the truth, I was furious of this woman in the Metropolitan who told you in front of Van Gogh painting, that he was insane, every time I feel we need to protect him. What it takes to be a child in our society, to believe in something what we can never learn to feel, to believe in human soul. In other words, Rembrandt also talked of human soul but never was foolish enough to trust it as much as Van Gogh did. This is why I look at Van Gogh to learn of his soul and I look at Rembrandt to learn of my soul.

Sonia G.

9/3/2015

Dear Professor,

Today i woke up with nausea and a light head, insomnia kept me from sleeping; so i won't be going in today. is there a way i can make up missed work?

thank you.
Leon

9/10/2015

Dear Professor,

Sorry I missed the first class! I was still working out my schedule. I look forward to seeing you tomorrow!

Thanks,
Sarah

9/11/2015

Dear Professor,

I am coming to class from a doctor's appointment that ran overtime so I will be late. Sorry in advance!

See you soon.
Thanks,
Sarah

10/2/2015

Dear Professor,

I apologize for missing class today. I'm going through a personal issue right now and it's overwhelming. This won't be something that will continue to happen, there's just a lot happening at this moment that demands immediate attention.
I know you didn't want this work e-mailed but I'll attach it anyway just so you know that I did it. I can bring a physical copy to class next week if that would be preferable.

Thank you and sorry for any inconvenience,
Terry E.

10/14/2015

Dear Professor,

I'm sorry for missing class last week. About an hour before class was meeting I got a call about the unexpected death of someone really important to me. I ended up going to be with my brother. I hope I can redeem the time I missed, is there any extra credit I could do?

Thank you,
John

10/15/2015

Dear Professor,

Good morning professor it's Leon, the guy who plays guitar from your class at 12:05 today. I haven't been in class this week and the end of last because i came down with the flu from my brother. I understand i haven't emailed you prior to notify so if the answer to my question is a no i understand. But is there any way i can hand in my essay when i get back? I've had it finished since you assigned it to us i just haven't been able to bring it in. If not i completely understand your rules and reasons.

Thank You.
Leon

10/30/2015

Dear Professor,

Obviously I never made it to last week's group in Chelsea.
As I think I told you, I had a "birthday luncheon" for an old friend at 1:30 – thought I'd be able to leave early, but there was no way I could walk out just when the "birthday fruit salad" (with one candle) was brought out – and I was way up on the East Side.
Got as far as 23rd Street at about 3:45 and realized I'd never find the group.

Tomorrow may be a repeat!
It's "Halloween Open House" at School of American Ballet – my chance to watch my favorite former NYC ballet dancers teach class.
If I can, I'll see you tomorrow-
If not, have a great weekend, and hopefully I'll see you next week.
Enjoy…..

Regards,
Sally

11/9/2015

Dear Professor,

Hope you are well. I was looking forward to today's class but, unfortunately, will not be able to attend due to a bout of bronchitis. I will miss you, but will focus on attending the next class. This has gone way too fast for me…wishing we had several more, because I can never get enough of your insights!

Warmly,
Deborah

11/18/2015

Dear Professor,

Not feeling well today...vertigo reoccurrence...so sorry to miss the last class of ████████...I loved the class...please keep me posted on your upcoming schedule...thank you... have a good holiday...

Josephine

Sent from my iPhone

12/3/2015

Dear Professor,

I wanted to inform you that I will not be in class tomorrow due to a family emergency, my grandmother is very ill. I will be back for the beginning of presentations next week, but I am leaving again on Wednesday, December 16th due to the same matter of health.

I apologize for the late correspondence, and I appreciate you understanding.

Best,

Jack

12/7/2015

Dear Professor,

Excuses section: I'm sorry that I had to leave early on Tuesday last week and was additionally unable to attend on Thursday. On Thursday something came up and I was sadly unable to attend any of my classes. For Tuesday I do not have such a good reason, if I am honest I left 20 minutes early because of a beautiful girl (the only and last time I would use this reason and I apologize, I let instinctual hedonism take over for better or worse!)

Interesting section: I have been working on this piece "To Fear with Love" and thought you might appreciate it as per our earlier discussion about writing. It is attached below for your enjoyment and I would love any feedback/criticism!

Best,
Abraham

3/10/2016

Dear Professor,

Unfortunately I won't make it to class today. Some logistical issues. Sorry to miss and see you next week,
Lois L.

Sent from my iPhone

3/14/2016

Dear Professor,

I am sorry to email you so last minute, but I will not be in class today. I woke up with a cold, and want to rest up as much as possible before traveling. So sorry.

Have a great spring break,
Sincerely,

Tilda B.

3/28/2016

Dear Professor,

Have been ill. Hope to attend class tomorrow. Assuming class assembles in ███████ as it did for 1st class (which I attended). Should I be late, could you leave info at desk as to which gallery you are starting in? Thank you Barbara B.

4/7/2016

Dear Professor,

Meant to e-mail you earlier –
I won't be at the ███████ on Thursday :(
I have an appointment with my dermatologist at 2:30 – un-
avoidable – his next opening is the first week in May!!!
Hopefully I'll be there next Thursday 4/14
Enjoy.

Regards,
Sally

4/15/2016

Dear Professor,

So there I was – albeit about 20 minutes late – at █████████.
Checked out the entire place – no group! I didn't love the exhibits – but figured you couldn't left that quickly!
It never dawned on me that I was in the wrong place! (I just looked at my calendar – I should have been at █████████ █████)!!!
Ah well … I'll go to █████ on my own during the week.
But as I strolled down Madison Avenue I decided not to let my geographical location go to waste – so I went to the new MET Breuer!
Loved some of those "unfinished" masterpieces!!!
Have a good week, and will hopefully see you next week.

Regards,
Sally

4/18/2016

Dear Professor,

I am requesting for an extension to complete all my missing assignments for your class. The reason for me missing work/class is because I was overwhelmed in this semester with my thesis and my personal issue with not having my grandmother, who I recently lost. My grandmother and I talked about my goals and what I have planned. I wanted to share and show my collection in honor of her name. And now she is not here to share this journey with which is hurting my academics. Please take this into consideration and will assure you I will complete all my assignments. I have already started research for my final presentation. I want to propose that the Guggenheim have a bi-annual exhibition for art students studying at any university in the city.

Thank you,
Jordan F.

4/18/2016

Dear Professor,

I hope you are well, I signed up for the Chelsea galleries wednesday event but unfortunately this past weekend my grandma passed away and I have been away since. I won't be back in time for the gallery tour, is there any other type of work I can do to make up for it or I can go and see the galleries by myself and write a reply on what I saw. Please do let me know, I'm so sorry for this inconvenience.

Best,

Mindy

5/31/2016

Dear Professor,

I'm really sorry but I won't be able to make it for the first class! I'm flying in from █████, and unfortunately had to change my flight due to some last-minute family issues.

I will be there from next week onwards! Please let me know what reading I can do to catch up.

Thank you!

Raquel C.

6/6/2016

Dear Professor,

Wondering if it might be possible for us to meet half an hour before or after the class this week for a quick walk-through/ catch-up of what I missed? If you could just take me through the period and artists covered, I can then read up on corresponding material.

Please let me know if that might be possible. Thank you!

Raquel C.

6/8/2016

Dear Professor,

I am so hoping not to miss class today because of the thunderstorms.

I will get ready and set out and hope that the rains do not stop me.

I am so looking forward!

With my warm wishes, Beverly M.

6/15/2016

Dear Professor,

I hope to be in class but I have had a virus on and off since last weekend. I have had not been feeling well on and off for several days and I so hope that I will feel up to class later as I know that it would cheer and inspire me.

For some reason, today my eyes seem to just want to close! If I am not at the Met on time, it means that I just felt that I need to stay home to try to get rid of this.

But if I don't make it, I will know that this is my loss!

Thank you for all that you offer me.

With best wishes, Beverly M.

6/15/2016

Dear Professor,

I fell asleep so I will have to miss your wonderful class today!

I lay down for a rest and all of a sudden woke up and so it would be hard to make class today.

I am so very sorry.

And if you feel like sending my good wishes to my classmates, that would be very very nice!

See you next week and be well.

Best from Beverly M.

8/13/2016

Dear Professor,

I am currently enrolled in your class ████████████████████
for Fall 2016 and am extremely excited to be enrolled in this class!

I am currently a ██████ student (████████████) and work full time in order to put myself through school. It can be extremely challenging to manage schedules and my priority is school, but sometimes work can get in the way. I usually wouldn't do this, but I am concerned with paying rent for this school year. I wanted to ask you if there is anyway I could miss the first class for an out of town work trip? Although I really hate missing the first class, my productivity would increase for the rest of the semester because going on this work trip would decrease my stress to pay rent on time. I know this is really not optimal and this is why I am emailing you. If there is any possibility for me to meet you outside of class in order to go over what I might be missing the very first class I would be very happy to do so. If you absolutely disagree with me missing the first class, I completely understand and will therefore make arrangements to stay in NYC that Friday. Please let me know what you think, so I can notify my employer.
Although this isn't the best introduction I am really thrilled that ████ is offering this course!

Thank you for your time

–Anne P.

9/21/2016

Dear Professor,

I started walking to the subway for our first class, but realized that the flu like virus that I have had since Sunday has not gone away and realized I need to stay at home, to my deep regret.

I have been looking forward for weeks and weeks to the start of the fall semester.

And while I don't want to impose too many details of my life, even though you are one of the most sensitive and compassionate teachers I have ever studied with, I truly hope that you do not mind my sharing a few things.

Suffice it to say that ███████████████████████████
██
██
██
██
██
██
██
██
██
██
██
███████████████████. I hope that you don't find this too crazy!!

I want to say that your class this summer was its highlight, ██
██
██████████! It is an honor and a privilege to study with you and be in your presence. You touch on the essence of the human condition and so many things that you say resonate so deeply

in my soul. Studying with you is like a spiritual experience for me. And I regret that I didn't fill out the summer course's evaluation in time as I would have said these things and more.

I will try to get to as many of your classes as I can this semester.

With my very best regards, Beverly M.

9/28/2016

Dear Professor,

Without going into details, suffice it to say that "no good deed goes unpunished!"

My care giving responsibilities have done me in, so I will have to miss another wonderful class.

Best always, Beverly M.

Author's Postface

8/24/2016

Dear Students,

I regret to inform you that tomorrow's class, Thursday, August 25, has been canceled. Due to personal reasons, I am still in Europe and unable to attend our first class.

I apologize for this last-minute cancellation and look forward to meeting you all September 1.

Best,

Professor Noterdaeme

Modest as our understanding of the human psyche and its realization in language and discourse is, one cannot but marvel at the unfathomable richness of this corpus of letters — despite belonging to the same genre (roughly described as apology letters), over the same medium (email), spanning six years, in the same language, mostly by individuals of the undergraduate age ("fair sprinkling of adults and senior citizens" notwithstanding), who were all enrolled in a couple or so of courses concerning the same overall subject matter and taught in no more than a couple or so of academic institutions of the same caliber and largely standardized (by state law) pedagogical and educational charter.

And yet this corpus of letters whisks us directly into the dilemma of personality and its realization in words, *sans* the comfortable distance of erudite jargon or clinical diagnosis. Those who believe that all of us are in essence the same will find here as much evidence to support their views as those who believe that we are all unique. Not unlike the debate whether photons are particles or waves, only those who will try to hold both horns of the bull in tandem will do justice to the data — provided they survive the experience.

Let's start with the sin of treating the whole book as one prolix letter and see what simple word frequency analysis can tell us about this average, intersex student. This sin is not only the most commonly committed one in psycho-linguistics, but also one of the very first and most influential in the field — making it a veritable "original sin."

Like many sins, word frequency analysis is aesthetically pleasing in a way that might sometimes cloud our judgment. Consider this word cloud of the entire book (In a word cloud, the size of the word is proportional to the frequency with which it is used):

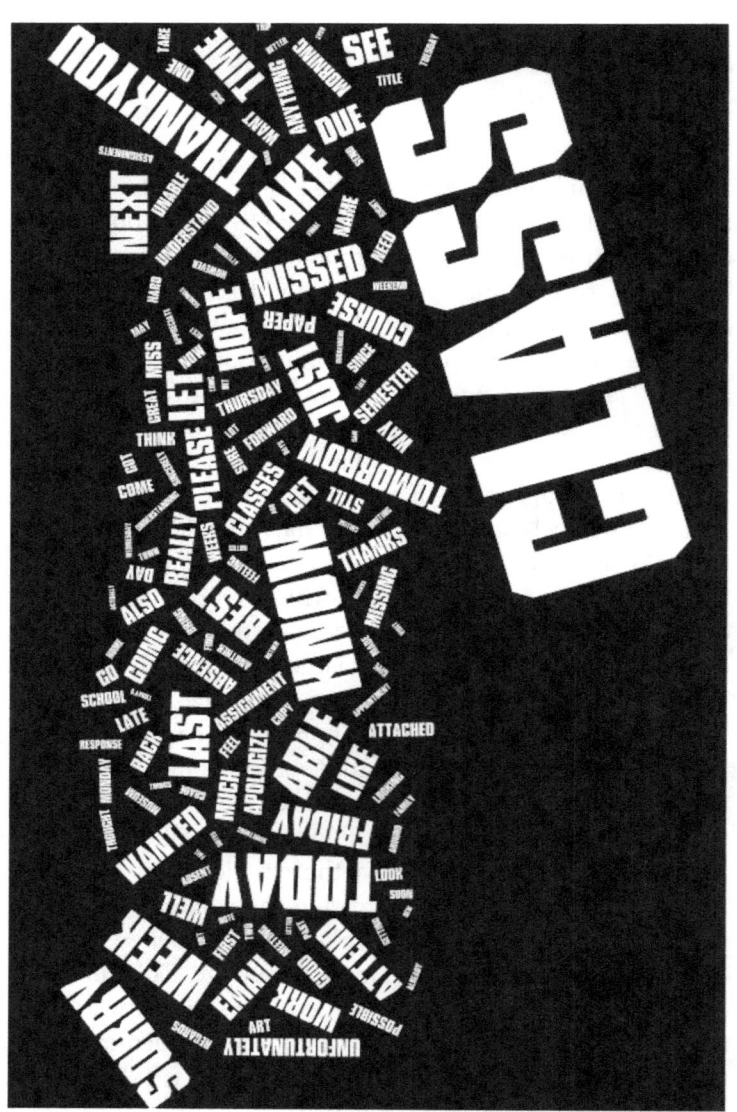

Our average, intersex student seems to be preoccupied with the word "class." The relative size of the word not only shows how much the concept (as an abstract noun, as a synonym for "course" or as a synonym for "session") looms large in the student's mind, but also how much it is "canonized" as a petrified concept, with no synonyms that could chip away at its size (consider, in contrast, the word "apologize" and how it might have diminished somewhat the size of "sorry" in the word cloud).

Yet the biggest deception of the word cloud is that it purports to show only "content" words, which supposedly carry "genuine" information. To do so, computational linguists of the "original sin" ilk discarded the bulk of the text, which is largely made of words they deemed uninformative: prepositions, pronouns, articles, and so on.

The ghosts of these words are haunting computational linguists to this day, but none more than the first person singular pronoun "I". Had I (here's this unescapable pronoun again!) added the word "I" to the word cloud above, it would have added an unseemly white block 4.5 times the size of the word "class."

Furthermore, one can claim that as our social landscape has become increasingly self-centered, self-authored, self-appointed, and self-promoted (in no small part due to the World Wide Web), it has accordingly been teeming with individual stories (with a demonstrable bias to success stories) and personal opinions (with a demonstrable bias to negative opinions) — all contributing to the abundance of the first person singular pronoun in the linguistic atmosphere around us. Inasmuch as this discourse particle is so prevalent as to feed off its own reflective energy and prevent the introduction of external perspective to the communicative sphere, then one might well consider it the prime culprit in a global linguistic climate change.

For all the self-centeredness of our mash-up student, the emails show remarkably low insight — if we are to believe the results of a thematic text analysis applied to the corpus. In thematic text analysis, all words that are synonymous, relevant or associated with a certain concept are tallied to gauge its prominence in the text. Using this technique we can ask "how many linguistic markers for insight do the emails contain? And what is the relative role of insight within the overall thinking of the writer"?

Considering the prominence of the single person pronoun in the emails, we may not be surprised to learn that "cognitive" words that are associated with reasoning and persuasion (e.g., "because," "but," "if," "just," "or," "since," etc. — all venerable building blocks of excuses) appear in 11.12% of the text (which is quite high for an interpersonal correspondence). After all, isn't the ultimate goal of this genre of emails to confess to a transgression while carefully choosing words that may minimize its damage? The surprising aspect of the emails is that the ratio of general cognitive (read: "excuse") words to "insight" words (e.g., words that show that the writer reflects back on their cognitive process: "believe," "conclude," "imagine," "perceive," "realize," "recognize," "think," "understand," etc.) is approximately 5 to 1. In other words, our composite student is on average at once cognitively sophisticated (as evidenced by the abundance of thinking-related words), self-absorbed (as evidenced by the abundance of single person pronouns), yet with little capability to reflect insightfully on their thinking and put it in larger perspective.

By now the reader of this epilogue might have a low opinion indeed of our composite student — and might have even proceeded to generalize this impression to all the students in the book (and beyond). This is a worthy experience to have — but not to trust. Though far messier than its computational counterpart, discourse analysis and its related fields (e.g., sociolinguistics, linguistic pragmatics, etc.) remind us that each individual may have different reasons for exhibiting similar verbal behavior. For example, what if the emails are low on insight because the professor is intimidating as to reduce the cognitive capacities of their students? Or what if the professor has an accent and the students are trying to minimize misunderstandings by choosing the most concrete language possible? (both examples were chosen for their distinct inapplicability to Prof. Noterdaeme).

Indeed, when one abandons the wholesale word counting and forays into the various ways in which the students in this book construct their sentences — even while expressing the same sentiment — the wholesome statistical picture quickly disintegrates into myriad hard-to-track idiosyncrasies. Let's revisit the first person singular pronoun and see what happens to it in context:

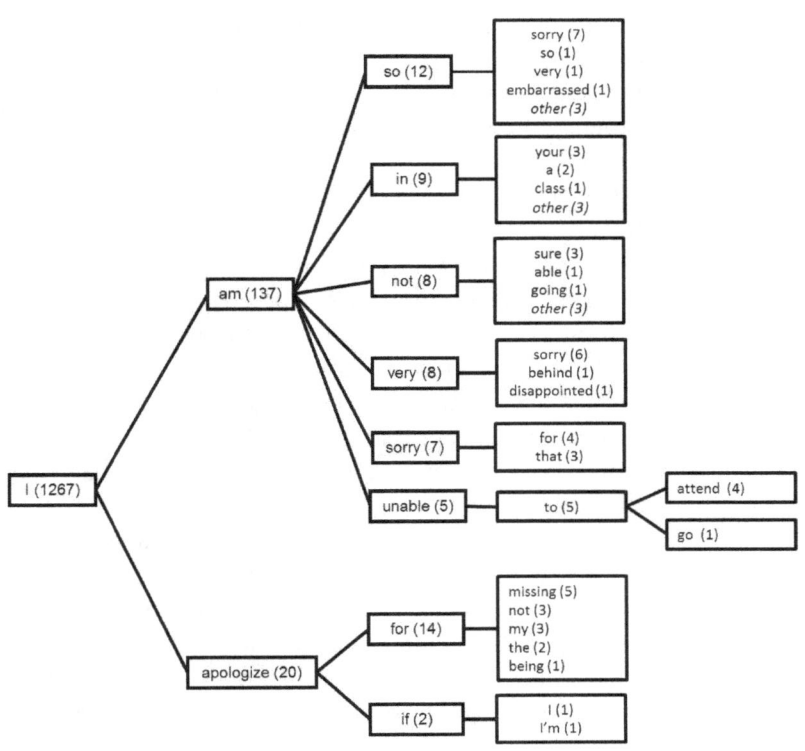

In other words, discourse analysis (or sociolinguistics) tell us that understanding word choice can hardly stop at their blind tallies. Rather, word choice can best be examined in their context, which may reveal the mental model that the individual writer has of their audience and the "tacit contract" that they follow in both form and content to express their minds. Consider this: both "I want(/ed) to let you know" and "I just want(/ed) to let you know" appear in the same frequency in the corpus (4 times). Generally speaking the modifier "just" is used mostly as a minimizer. If so, what exactly is the writer trying to minimize by choosing (not necessarily consciously) to write "I just wanted you to know", and how is that (in their mind, at least — and again, not necessarily consciously) more effective in conveying their intentions than "I wanted you to know"? Considering the tremendous variability with which people may convey roughly the same idea and how this variability is linked with their (conscious, unconscious, or anywhere in between) assumptions about how the world works or what make their professor "tick" may just as easily make this book a meditation on individuality.

Such are the preoccupations of the conscientious linguist, and they don't spare the writer of these lines. Is the tone of the epilogue too didactic, I wonder? And if it is, is it because I grew up with two idealistic educators as parents? Perhaps. Or is it because I have a congenital disposition towards being didactic? Equally likely. Or maybe I tailored this epilogue to the readership of this book, which is a projection of my own students? Also likely. Or perhaps it's all of the above? Or maybe I just don't know since not all my linguistic motives are available to me consciously.

This innate uncertainty in language may seem daunting and despairing, and with the dramatic improvement in computational power and storage capacities, it sometimes looks as if we are so grateful to quantitative methods for sorting out our messy world into simpler, manageable, reproducible, and standardized categories (and doing it so efficiently and rapidly, without ever complaining!) that we might be confusing gratitude with servitude, and forget that these categories are still ultimately but a simplification of our own messy perceptions — and sometimes an arbitrary simplification at that. Let's hope that whoever judges us based on a computerized version of our word choice (NSA, anybody?) does not lose sight of this fact.

In contrast, psycho- and sociolinguists, along with philosophers and other scholars, have been laboring over these fundamental discursive forces for decades, with no decisive hierarchy. Do speakers craft their sentences based on the norms they grew up on? Or based on the norms that they observe around them (whether in real life or through the "realities" of the entertainment industry)? Do they primarily strive to align the information with what they think the listener already knows and is capable or expecting to hear? Or do they primarily strive to minimize the possibility that the listener will feel slighted or stupid? And so on. Each approach proved a fertile (though admittedly messy) ground not only for a new variation of discourse analysis but also for whole linguistic sub-fields and "cliques." As much as it may frustrate those who would like to see the field of discourse analysis become standardized and canonized as its quantitative and computational counterparts, its real-life messiness is more akin to the merry mayhem that ensues when a diverse group of creatures play cricket together, and so I would encourage the reader to apply the Dodo bird verdict as featured in *Alice's Adventures in Wonderland*: "Everybody has won, and all must have prizes."

Dr. Shuki Cohen, MSc, PhD
John Jay College of Criminal Justice
New York, NY

"W. dreams, like Phaedrus, of an army of thinker-friends, thinker-lovers. He dreams of a thought-army, a thought-pack, which would storm the philosophical Houses of Parliament. He dreams of Tartars from the philosophical steppes, of thought-barbarians, thought-outsiders. What distance would shine in their eyes!"

— Lars Iyer